T0143007

Different
FACES

Different
FACES

Marlene Essence Dotts

DIFFERENT FACES

iUniverse books may be ordered through booksellers or by contacting:

iUniverse
1663 Liberty Drive
Bloomington, IN 47403
www.iuniverse.com
1-800-Authors (1-800-288-4677)

Because of the dynamic nature of the Internet, any web addresses or links contained in this book may have changed since publication and may no longer be valid. The views expressed in this work are solely those of the author and do not necessarily reflect the views of the publisher, and the publisher hereby disclaims any responsibility for them.

Any people depicted in stock imagery provided by Getty Images are models, and such images are being used for illustrative purposes only.
Certain stock imagery © Getty Images.

ISBN: 978-1-5320-8592-5 (sc)
ISBN: 978-1-5320-8593-2 (e)

Library of Congress Control Number: 2020903702

Print information available on the last page.

iUniverse rev. date: 02/24/2020

God grant me the *Serenity* to accept the things I
cannot change, the *Courage* to change the things
I can and the *Wisdom* to know the Difference.

God, I place my hand in yours and together
we can do something good....

I can't do it alone!

ROAD TO REHAB

It was a hot summer day in July 2018 when I checked myself into a rehab in Paterson, New Jersey. I had never been to a rehab before I left Long Branch, New Jersey three days earlier. I had left everyone…family, friends, so called anyhow. When I stepped on to the train, I slowly looked back to wave goodbye to my husband, Chris, who had been sick for some time with heart and reno failure. We had been together since 1996 and married in 2001. We then separated in 2007. We were to go our separate ways. It was in 2007 when life's challenges happened. I had grandkids being brought into the world. Knowing in my heart that I already failed as a parent, I wanted to be there for my grandkids. I knew my kids would need their mother so I had to make a choice: get sober or continue to use drugs and alcohol. In order to make better choices, I needed to be separated from my husband because he was my enabler. He couldn't tell me, "no." He was a good guy, but on the down side he could be very mean and abusive. I tried to get sober on my own.

As I was sitting on the train while it was pulling off, I recalled hearing the conductor say, "We are now approaching Monmouth Park and Little Silver is next." My heart started palpitating and my eyes began filling with tears. I thought of saying, "STOP!" I did not want to go through with this. This would be a whole new way of life for me. Part of me knew inside that God would be giving me a new chance to live a more abundant life but another part of me was afraid to take this leap of faith. I thought to myself, "I should just get off in Middletown." I had an acquaintance, Mr. D, that lived there. I thought he would let me stay there…I could get high…. but something kept me on that train. My mind was all over the place. I had already made the arrangement for my daughter, Tiarrah to meet me in Newark Penn Station. I guess reality started setting in, thinking to myself, "How could this happen?" My daughter was taking off work to take me to a rehab and for me not to show up would be a real disappointment and another slap in her face. I already felt like a failure. "Why can't I just get life right...Why can't I just live a normal life!" Tears were flowing down my face uncontrollably after passing through Middletown. There was no turning back for me now. I was determined to get back into my own apartment, which was, at the time, my main goal and I thought, "the hell with everyone else."

FIRST FEW DAYS OF REHAB...JULY 2018

I felt lost, angry and confused. My mind raced with so many thoughts. So much had happened and I didn't understand why. All I did know was that I had to go to this fucking rehab to get my life back. I had lost everything; my apartment, my job, my daughters and my grandkids. At the time, I didn't want to accept any blame on my part. I thought to myself, "I don't have a problem; I didn't hurt anyone...Yeah, I got evicted, lost my apartment and everything that was on the inside was now on the outside." I was furious with my landlord for not working with me. I also believed it wasn't my fault that I didn't pay rent or didn't call him to make payment arrangements because in my mind, I had it *all* under control. I took all 6 of my grandkids and one of their friend that lived in the same building as me on a 3 day road trip to Orlando florida for christmas, i figured i'll pay rent when i get back, well hell income tax is the following month as i thought, i had no idea what i had in store for me.before i started in the road trip to florida i purchased food, water, candy and drugs yes i had drugs on this road trip how insane was that..i didn't think it was insane with kids in the car, we got stopped once thank god the police officer didn't ask to search the car of course james got a ticket for driving too close to another car, james was driving and i'm yelling at him to stop getting close to other cars, eventually i took over, at rest stops i would use in the bathrooms to stay awake, telling this story thinking on that time i could've got caught and my kids and neighbor thinking their children were safe, we made to florida and spent christmas there it was a fun time, i ran out of drugs, thinking about how i couldn't wait to get back home, i felt so drained just wanting to sleep..oh boy i fell asleep james used the car to go to the store i didn't know, all i know is that he woke me up to say he hit another car, he left note on the guy car and said i hit your car please call me james left my phone to call, i ran outside to examine the car, the car that was rented now have a dent in the car the other car was more damaged.This whole trip cost me five thousand dollars renting a van for seven days, food, gas, renting 2 villas and now the accident..i should've paid rent. The rent I said I would pay income tax time..the car rental took that out my account... boy i'm thinking this is bad, so now i have a little back up plan, i had money on the money app.it's now march and here comes the eviction letter i had money saved but now cant get the money off," the company deactivated my account with all my money on it!" I started asking god for help, I could have asked for help when i left him again. Once again, I had to go to court and once I again I lost. I remember going to Mr. D's house and crying myself to sleep. I was still trying to find a way to fight but by this time my car got repossessed. went to court with some money, the court would, not accept it, i had just that day to come up with the money, the next day i took the realtor most of the money they weren't there so i dropped it in the mailbox, they called me and wouldn't accept, when i finally got my money off the app it was to late and the landlord sent my money back to me.i begged and pleaded for him to take the money i been in this apartment for five years and he said no, it felt like my heart was coming up through my throat, i asked why..he said that i had people living with me, but it hasn't never been a problem before with my daughter living there, he also said that one of my daughter friends was intoxicated and we to someone else house trying to get in the neighbor had to call the cops, he said i just gave my apartment cause i was never there.

When I got into rehab my first day there was a nightmare, first i thought they took us to the store to get food, hair and nail done, im thought that when got upstair it was a relief going through all the processing, i was tired i figured i'll make my bed and go to sleep that wasn't the case, yeah i made my bed and i had to group..i said to myself i'm not going to no group i'm tired but i had no choice but to go, before turning in that night i got on my knee and cried, i couldn't catch my breath tears are pouring at this point the feeling of loneliness and fears asking god to please help me, i was really lost i was stripped down to nothing, no family, no car, no apartment, no friends the only one thing i had left was prayer and i didn't even know that maybe god turned his back on me too. Day 2, i woke up yelling for someone to get the nurse, the nurse came running in the room, she asked what was going on, i said i can't move i can't get out of bed, the look she gave me, if looks could kill i'll be dead she looked at me with disbelief and said maybe this isn't the place for you, i mentioned to her that my SAI worker said yall would help me with my condition, my back injury, everyone same running to my room looking in..how embarrassing this is as i thought i said oh god i can't do this tears are dripping down the sides of my face one of my roommate helped me get out of bed, i can't believe this nurse left me there i managed to get up and make my bed, i thought to myself i alway had somebody to help me out of bed..this is horrible! How am I going to manage this? We had group 3rd day of rehab, I attended a group session and listened to others share.

When it came to my turn, I told the others about my drug of choice and why I needed to be there. I explained how this was my first time in rehab. I heard myself saying, "I guess it was meant for me to be here." I came with no intentions of making friends and wanted no drama. I was there to try to figure out the rest of my life, what my future would hold and how this would be totally up to me. Deep in my heart, I began thinking; "God has a plan for me." I began to feel some hope. I began accepting that God actually loves me because he saved me from myself as well as others.

As I reflected about my past, I knew I needed to be saved. I had so much anger. There was nothing but chaos.

CHRONICLES OF MY PAST: MY ROLLER COASTER LIFE BEFORE REHAB...

"Money..Sell..." I had drugs, men, money, a little crazy white bitch who asked me to pimp her out. I thought it was going to be easy, just slap her around and have her make my money. But it didn't turn out that way. She was a sheep in wolves clothing. She was a good thief and I had a driver, who delivered for me. I was a queen pimp and my whole team were all men, my dealers, my driver, my housekeeper... all men. It was a 24/7 job and it was nice, so I thought until I got caught. It was months after I met Mr.

D through my daughter's boyfriend. At first I thought Mr. D would be a good connection for me but Mr. D had it all wrong! In time, he was also getting out of control stealing from me and thought I didn't know it. I could've had him beat up or I could've clearly done it myself. I rationalized with myself that I didn't want violence although I could have cut his throat when he put an order in.

I was just too nice to people, especially when it came to the drugs and the street life. Back to white girl blue who asked me to pimp her. I knew the basics for me were to send her out, get money and collect… and that was that. I had to slap her a few times when she kept stealing. After a while I gave up and let her go. I also had to slap Terry at one time when he was trying to get over on me. I guess I was on a slapping spree, trying to conduct business by myself and trying to maintain motherfucker, James. He was still around, protecting me, making sure no one messed with me but then James went to jail. At this point, everything went south for me. I believed if he hadn't gone to jail, things wouldn't have gone the way they did. Terry began stealing from me. At times I trusted James, but in way I just hated when I woke up and everything would be misplaced or he would take my stuff with him. I would call him so angry, "Where are you!! And bring me my shit!"

In just a month, he had no money and my money was stacking up. I moved out of my apartment that I shared with my daughters and her three kids, her boyfriend and my mom. I was gone most of the time anyway but still had checked in sometimes. I moved in with Terry because his girlfriend had a stroke. I continued my business there. As long as I got Terry high, he was fine. I also did the food shopping, making sure there was food in the house and also kept the house clean. I still had my driver who was delivering for me and driving me where I needed to go. I also spent a lot of time with Mr. D. When I needed rest, I could go there and escape from the world and isolate myself, which I was good at. I would "hide" from family, bill collectors, and others I needed to get away from. Isolation was my best friend.

After awhile, I tried to distance myself from Mr. D when he started trying to run my life, telling me what to do. I felt that nobody tells me, "the queen-bee," what or how to do shit. Nevertheless, Mr. D still brought a lot of money in more ways than one. I believed he was one of my tickets. When I got drugs, he wanted to sample them and would send money back with my driver.

There has also been another person in my life at the time, Terry. Terry was like a brother to me but that was not always a good thing. Terry and I were driving to Mr. D's house to shower and change clothes. On the way, Terry and I stopped at the store to get cigarettes and a lighter. As I pulled out of the parking lot, the police were right behind me. I knew right away that they were going to stop me. When I saw their lights turn on, I was thinking, "How can I get out of this shit?" The officer pulled me over and asked me for my license, registration & insurance. I told them my license was suspended but I had to take Terry to the hospital. That excuse didn't work. I started arguing with the officer when he said they were going to need to search the car. It was either I let them search or they were going to call in for the dogs to search. I really had no choice, so I allowed them to search the car. They first found 12gms of crack cocaine and then they found the heroin. I felt like this was the end for me. I was done. I knew I was going to jail.

Although I never used heroin, I sure acted like I did when I got to the jail. I had recognized some of the guards that worked in the jail. I was so taken back when one of the guards was a family acquaintance that I knew since she was a young girl. Now here she was asking me to drop my underwear, squat and cough. I said to myself, "Oh God… I'm too old for this shit. I need to give this mess up…"

I spent two days in the county jail before seeing the judge. I was let out on bail reform, which meant that I had to report once a week in Freehold to be monitored and give urine. I also had to call in once a week to make sure I got no new charges.

During the days that I was incarcerated, Terry had all my money, th in the back seat of his car which was the money i got back off the app and what the landlord gave me back Prior to my arrest, I had helped Terry get a motel room after we both had been evicted on the same day but then he went on to blame me for it. It was crazy that he accused me of selling drugs out of his apartment. When he was in the hospital, he wanted somebody to blame and it was me.

As soon as I was released, I called my cousin Mark to pick me up. He took me to get something to eat and then we drove to Eatontown to go find Terry. When we got to Terry's hotel room, the door was open so I went in to wait for him to come back as he was nowhere to be found. I was sitting on the bed and the motel attendant came in and told me to leave. Terry took all of my money. This is how he repaid me for trying to help him. I couldn't believe it. Mark then dropped me off at my husband Chris's sister's house. Chris had been staying there but they wouldn't let me stay. I called my Aunt Phyllis and she came to get me and let me stay the night at her house. Before she got there, I told my husband, "you too helped me get evicted and you can't even help me stay or get me a room?" I couldn't believe this was happening to me. I was to fucking through with him, Terry and most of the people in my life.

I truly believed at this time I should've fallen onto my knees and pray but I just couldn't. I didn't care because at the time, so much shit was slapping me in the face. I still couldn't admit that I was powerless and my life had become so unmanageable.

Once again, I had to go to court and once I again I lost. I remember going to Mr. D's house and crying myself to sleep. I was still trying to find a way to fight but by this time my car got repossessed.

The next thing I could remember was when my daughters, Tiarrah, Ashley and Ebony decided to do an intervention. They were all yelling at me. I was looking at each of them and they were all sounding like Charlie Brown's teacher to me. I went into another room, closed the door and felt like I was a failure once again. I fucked up. In my anguish, I started to get high. I paced the floor, cursing and thinking about how everybody thinks they are better than me. Thoughts were flooding my head.... "What's the difference... when you get evicted and when you have no control over what happens...

I also was in a financial crisis. I had a financial account that was deactivated. Again I thought it was probably meant to happen this way so God could get me alone and get me away from people who didn't give two shits about me.

I didn't trust most of the people around me so I went back to Chris who I hoped could get me out of this mess. Now I have a warrant of removal - court date. I was still thinking my cousin was going to give me my money back, which was about $800. My account had been deactivated because the car rental company took $2,000 out of my account from an accident of the rental car we had while in Florida. The company had sent me an email stating the reason for the deactivation was due to a dispute about a transaction because there were disputes regarding my business. I sent them everything they needed and asked for, i did that they said the money would be in my bank account the next day, then they send me an email stating if customer was dispute any charges they would have to give their money back, i'm thinking people who buy food don't dispute charges, in my mind i'm thinking wow, people are swiping their credit cards for drugs and i had to make up receipt to make it seem that i was selling food. I thought, "Oh boy... what else can go wrong?" A whole lot of shit went left for me.

In the group today I was sharing about the pain I caused people that i didn't think would be harmed i also shared that my husband Chris was getting healthy and I saw how he really fought for his life. I had then been with James so it was going to be hard for me to now go back to him. While Chris was sick I had left him messages and would send him clothes and care packages. I knew that wasn't enough, then I thought we were not together but I also knew he loved me, at this point I loved no one, not even myself.as i shared and i listened to other share, i didn't realize the pain i caused my husband and how i was so selfish to turn on him while he was in the hospital, i felt so shameful all that i've done is in my face, i can't run nor hide from it.can i justify or rationalize, i thought this i had to come face to face with this with being honest to myself as well as others, i continue to share my story about what happened before i came into the rehab.

Now my back was against the wall. It hurt me that I had to resort back to Chris for help. In my heart I knew it was the wrong choice among the many wrong choices I had made that were causing me to drown. Why did I think he would help me after what I did? Surprisingly he said he would help me but that was after he threw a 1/2 lb. of marijuana onto my lap. All I knew was I needed the help even though I also knew that I should start slowing down. I had been hearing my name too much in the street. I knew the cops had to be watching me. I was constantly getting stopped or pulled over. The money was slowing down and so was I. But I had to keep a flow to make sure I was able to keep getting high.

Thinking back to when I got back home from a trip to Florida and all that detoxing I was doing while there went out the window. I had too many addictive personalities beside me. I was using cocaine and selling marijuana, heroin and crack cocaine. My addictions increased my sex drive and I had started to lose weight from steaming everyday. I was looking good in a size 12-14. I never thought in a million years I would ever see that size. I was steaming and exercising in the bathroom. I would run the hot water in the shower and let the bathroom get steamed up. A person started asking me how I was losing so much weight and I told them how I was steaming. I know what people were probably really thinking but I didn't care and didn't give a shit what they were thinking about me. When I died, they were still going to talk. So, from a size 18-20 to a size 12-14, I was definitely drawing lots of attention. I was fitting into clothes that I had in my closet for 2 years that still had tags on them. I started to feel I was getting control back in my life.

TODAY A ONE ON ONE WITH MY COUNSELOR

My counselor asked me how my relationship with my oldest daughter I began to explain to her that my daughter's life was not stable, which was not good for her boys. Thinking that I had things under control, I wanted to take care of her boys and get a roof over their heads. I went to court and got resident custody of them since she had nowhere to go. I wanted to give them a stable home. She thought I was trying to take them away from her but I just wanted some stability for them. It wasn't my intention for her not to be with them. Because she didn't understand this, she threatened to fight me, calling me a bitch and other names. We kept going back and forth to court because she was trying to get other family members to take the boys. Different family members started turning against me. I was angry with this and couldn't understand how anyone in their right mind would want to see kids homeless. She couldn't take care of her kids at that time. People would get jealous. Some people did not want to see me doing better than them.

When the case was brought in front of a judge, he didn't want to hear it I was their biological grandmother, the judge ordered DYFS to come out to my house to do inspection my apartment they felt my home was a stable environment the boys they had everything they needed their own room, when my daughter got her new apartment we went back to court I gave her 2 boys back but it was long before they were homeless again. The total years I had them were 5-6 years I wasn't nothing that they didn't want or have.

I guess all the bickering and going back and forth the court for my grand boys and all I wanted was for them to have a home. He came home 2 every day and did not have to wonder where they were going to sleep. My daughter Ebony didn't see it that way. I was every name in the book I was called bitches I was threatened by her not just her but by other people saying I was wrong. Well a year later history repeated itself she gets evicted again. Then her boyfriend hits me in the head with a chair cause I tried helping them getting food he asked can he borrow money he got upon his feet he had a new job but haven't enough funds to get back and forth to work seen no problem with it I gave the boys back to ebony I no longer tried to fight her in court all I wanted was for the boys to have a home I excited they get a new apartment in Newark NJ had a new baby girl, we were drinking and cooking I cooked oxtails collard green baked macaroni and cheese, he was want to bet money on a race on who can run the fastest between him and my daughter's boyfriend, I said if you can bet money you can pay me what you owe me all I can remember was him putting his finger in my face and I retaliated he picked up a chair, hit me in the head, I called the police, they were so slow coming he ran, things wasn't the same after that and my daughter stayed with him that hurt me the most I was her mother and she allowed this man to pick up a chair and hit me with there's no way I would've stayed with no man that hit my mom, new baby or one months prior to this me and daughter had just reconciled our differences. This incident caused a lot of problems for me and I started to use it again.i couldn't understand that she stayed with a man that hit her mother, i couldn't do that there's that much love in the world no matter what my mom has ever done to me i wouldnt have ever, e and my mom would have jumped him, then called the police, i continue on explaining no matter i ever done just was good enough for her or anyone, she was living with me and knew my situation and no one help me keep my apartment everyone just talked about me, including my mom, i went on to say if everyone would help me pay the rent we could have still been there and i have gotten the money off the app, i would have repaid everyone back, i believe that this was god's plan to get me out of this situation, everyone was just stabbing me in the back, i sighed with tears in my eyes.My counselor said with a reply your safe, you're on your way to a new journey of your life, she never really have to much to say, i guess i have to figure out the rest along the way, feel that i have to start sharing with her, i was going to a one on one and didn't say much she just wasn't talking the same language as i was..i kept ask her what was going on the my progress, where was i going from this rehab, she never had a solution.

So, I couldn't believe I'd relapsed, this time Chris didn't know, I did it one night I won't go back, I felt nothing was really going on in my life I guess it was playing with fire I have a habit of that love getting burnt the fuck up knowing it bad but do it anyway.

After the night was over I went back to my daily activity and that was I had to put my Dotts family reunion together that we did every year no one liked the idea at the last minute of having it at the beach in Long Branch N.J and the family members who did put their money in I made everything happen. D.J. food etc. we had a good time. It's always good to see the elders come out and enjoy themselves and of course I get drunk and act a fool again right in Chris face I tried talking to a guy that my cousin brought with him that was some bold shit Chris will kick ass ask question later. But I felt like we weren't together, guess after my ex passed away I never had a chance to mourn him right after his funeral I had a Mothers Day stripper party set up prior to him passing away so the day of his funeral I had to do this party it was already paid for, after the party I was already intoxicated we cleaned the hall after the party, me, lil sis and teeny went to murphy bar in long branch, went to the bathroom fell to my knees, it was a cry I just couldn't catch my breath, Teeny walked in the bathroom picked me up and said come on Tink you can't do this. I guess that's when I just stop caring, but what really hit the fan is when I got into the car accident and couldn't work or get out of bed my legs started giving out on me, like I would just fall for no reason at the hospital in long branch got me as fall risk. aAt this time is where i started really feeling depressed, i couldn't get of bed i couldn't do the thing i was doing, my friends and i was go out dancing and i couldnt, what hurts the most is that people didn't believe me, like i needed to lie, one day my nephew mom came over we always use to hang out, she seen me take a step forward and fell, tis was really a turning point for me Remember when I said my husband can say no to me, my enabler, well I talked him into selling cocaine so he did I needed money and remember when I said I was over a friend's house and I relapsed well there I went back to using and using was my go to, cause everyone thought I was faking when my back and my legs was really hurt I was in so much pain. i guess by me sharing these incidents that occured prior to me relapsing and while i was relapsing, i see people were really listening, in groups that all i needed was for one to hear my cries, just listen and feel what i was going through i started to come around, a hug goes a long way even though in this rehab we weren't aloud to hug but the right words of encouragement meant a lot even after i said i didn't want to meet people, i came to this rehab angry and bitter of course i didn't make the right choices that lead me here, now i'm faced with drug charges and i don't know how im going to make out with that i got caught twice in a week, i know im facing jail time, often wonder how much time, ONE DAY AT A TIME!

I often laid in bed just thinking about what I could've done or said differently. I started to think of this moment when I was intoxicated. The time before when he got sick, his girlfriend from when we split up she was waiting for him to die thinking she was going to get nothing! Dumb ass broad! He was still married to me!

It wasn't doing long before I joined him, but didn't deserve to be his punching bag ..hell no! I asked his girlfriend cause on this day I was drunk and I asked her has Chris hit you when she said no oh boy was I angry and I said to him with her sitting at his sister's house you never hit this white Italian bitch but you'll hit me I knew I would never go back to Chris I will be there for him, help him, I will never take him back I told him to slap the shit out her everybody on the room stopped and looked! "Yup that's what I said" I repeated myself I said Chris slap the shit out of her! Chris 2 sisters Donna & Renee stood and looked with disbelief and started cracking up his ex-turned red in the face seemed like she wanted to cry. She didn't know what to expect from me. i often wonder was i that bad of a person for him to attack me, sometimes for no reason when we were together i had to watch what i said or how i said things i've always been an out spoking person and refuse to allow someone to take that away from me as I'm standing there with my armed folded drunk filled with anger emotions wanting to fight because I am wondering why he hasn't fucked her up like he did me. And I'm his wife oh that right I never called the police and she would've and she's white they would've hung his ass.

Just when you thought you've taken care all your legal shit more legal shit arises I spent days in jail after going in front of the judge for the old warrant in 1994 he gave me time served if I was to do 7 more days so I ask my friend, she was like a sister to me to go the court and pay the fine for me so I could get out, I was out by the next day.

I was cool and I went back to work like nothing happened. My friend got me out on a bail bond on the other charges. I'm happy out of jail free.

But it didn't take me too long before I got back in the selling of the marijuana again - now I have bills, rent, bond man car note and Ins. Cause after the accident on July 30 2017 I got really depressed I couldn't walk, I needed help getting out of bed and I needed people and I think I am young for this. I was getting life back with sciatica, now its worst. The accident made it worse! I don't want to paint an ugly picture of Chris. He was a good guy to have put up with my shit as well.

Back in somehow so he moved back in to help me with the boys under the circumstances no strings attached life still kind of OK I'm selling marijuana working 1 patient and that was just driving that 1 patient to the grocery store while she shop I didn't have to do anything but help put groceries in the car and take them out the car how easy that was, but oh shit, shit wasn't great I got caught with 19 bags of marijuana and 8 Xanax on July 4 2017, this was the life. I was working for lyft

Got pulled over for making a turn on red, the officer ran my name I had a fucking warrant from 94 for Christ sakes you got to be kidding me. Of course, I get arrested and what is found in my purse. I was crying telling the officer I don't know how it got in my purse. It wasn't a mind. And I knew damn well it was mine. I was so tired and forgot to check my purse before leaving home how dumb!

I had gotten this Chevy Malibu 2011 I so loved that car during the time of me putting down the crack cocaine I got my high school diploma while in adult high school I'm in medical assistant school I graduate adult high on my birthday June 6 2010 the I graduated medical right after, I did pursue the career as a medical assistant but I started working in elderly and disabled peoples home and I loved my job I was doing this job for 7 year. Until one day my back started bothering me I went to the hospital they said I had Sciatica and it came from lifting a patient I we prescribed medication for it and therapy I was feeling OK until July 30 2017 a car hit me from behind all my grandkids were in the back seat all strapped in all 5 of my grandboys. Z y' heir, & Z y' Meir William, Ty'Quell Walker, Daviyon Alexander, and lil Rayquan Purnell and one of their friends and my daughter Ashley Cassidy was in the front seat. The next day I couldn't get out of bed then I knew something was wrong I went to the hospital I told them I was in a car accident the day before I didn't feel pain where I had to go to the hospital after the accident Things started getting really bad for me and Chris knew I need help he always found his way back, after 10 years of being sober from cocaine this accident really put me in depression,

My house got raided of course I took like weight got a fine, but I wasn't long before I was back and it again how bitter than I was. Now I with the husband whom have just living in my home and I still running toward wealth the ex-boyfriend what a fucking 3 mg circus.

I can say that I always needed my husband even though my husband was an asshole he was a sweet with a bitter sweet, when he was sweet he brought me flower we would go out to dinner he was a sweet nice guy but when he was enraged it wasn't no stopping him when we would fight you can see the anger that scared me because that much anger sometimes when a person just keeps hitting you, you can help but to wonder is he going to stop or is he going to kill me he's a Zebra cause zebra don't lose their stripes, he was very abusive mentally and physically I stayed in the past he had what I wanted and that was drugs I didn't want to sell my ass for it a go stealing as long as I stayed I was safe so what he treated me like shit sometimes or beat the hell but me I just wanted to get high. Even when I took him back I wasn't use crack I was 10 years sober from using crack cocaine, he said he changed it was long before the Zebra lost his stripes then I know I just couldn't do it no more a month before I really was trying to make my marriage work and letting go of the ex. Now I had 3 car my very first car was a Saturn no one couldn't drive because it was a stick shift my husband got me to trade in my car for a better car I had a Mazda 5 MiniVan he use the van to go to store, I get a phone and its him telling me my car is crashed when I got the site where the car was crashed I ran pat him to see my car was stuck to an electricity pole it was totaled the ambulance took him the hospital thank god he's was alright 2 weeks later I got another car Chevy Malibu 2011 it was clean with very little mileage on it.

Alcohol had me very promiscuous, passing out, black outs then I went to sell marijuana I didn't use marijuana, so I figured me and my stinking thinking boy, life was great I'm getting drunk sell to marijuana, life was good, I'm throwing parties, the party girl! Popping perks, E pills. going to clubs.

Then people start seeing me for what I was. a drunken clown, a whore. My boyfriend was embarrassed to even go out in public with me. I would curse him the next morning he would tell me, and I would remember. The disappointment in his face left me curious to wonder what did they say a drunk person speaks a sober mind but on the he allowed things to happen to me that shouldn't have happen and it really frustrated me, like the night when my brother punched me in my face which had broken my ankle

uncle if he would've put him and his girlfriend out the car that incident wouldn't have happened after I went to the hospital from getting surgery on my ankle my own mother didn't even call to check on me, she can to my house to arguing with about some crock pot she let me borrow, boy she really show her different face she started to tell me oh your brother didn't do that to you I told her to get out my fucking house when it came to me she didn't give two shits about me where he was there and didn't protect me, so I felt so type of way about that so drinking alcohol let the beast out! Marlene was sweet without it! That was an abusive and toxic relationship he drank despite of it all I loved him when guy came up to me I would flirt back I guess just to get him upset I knew at some point I was wrong I never got a reaction what kind of reaction was I looking for. I guess love and support reactions I didn't see. We winded up splitting up year or a little less than a year I watched him take his last breath. Days prior to him dying we went out to dinner we both ordered our food he had soda and I ordered wine we talk and I asked him did he forgive me, I felt I really owed him an apology and I did apologize and so did before not being there for me I seen people taking advantage of him I would say something he'd never listened I didn't know that this was going to be the last time is at down and ate dinner with him, we went down to Atlantic city to visit my pastor and first lady I call them mom & pop, I was talking to him all that day nothing seemed different about him, as I'm leaving Atlantic city I get a phone call from his sister that he was in the hospital, I asked her what was wrong she didn't know I told her I was coming from Atlantic city and I be there shortly it wrecked me I didn't haven't, whatever it was it wasn't enough I'm understanding to what happen I wanted to die with him, remembering going to church at this time I'm active in church, after being active in church I read in the bible you can drink not to be foolish, foolish was me I still drank not to the point of passing out and going on rampages I guess I was looking for answers I never got the answers I was looking for when or why he died like that, I remember going to church and speaking with the pastors wife when I spoke to about it she didn't say what I needed to hear there I turned away from god, I stopped going to church at this time my husband is living with me, that when everything started to fall apart for me.

Somehow I found myself sitting in welfare trying to get "GA" (General Assistance) and trying to get shelter. I wanted to go to a hotel room because I had my cat, Brandy, with me but the worker said they don't put people in hotels any more and in order for me to go into the shelter I had to get GA assistance. I began the application, which was an all-day process. They offered to put my Brandy into an animal shelter. I didn't feel comfortable about me being separated from Brandy. At first it seemed that they wouldn't be able to help me because I have gotten evicted. After some more paperwork, they eventually offered the shelter to me but I didn't take it because they would take Brandy from me. They offered to have me talk to a SA worker. I agreed but really did not know what an SA worker was. When I asked, I was told an SA worker helped with substance abuse. I thought about it and decided to make an appointment.

One of the social workers called my aunt to find out if I could stay with her, they call family members to see if a family member would take you in before going into the shelter, the social worker came back out to the waiting room and informed me my aunt was coming to pick me up..i was uughhh nothing seems to be going my way today..not wanting to going onto a shelter so I guess my next option was to go with my aunt, didn't want too! SO my aunt came to pick me up and who she had in the car with her..my husband she asked him to ride with her to pick me up, she decided to let me stay with her as long as I let my other cousin take Brandy. It was hard for me to leave Brandy with my cousin because I felt like she was my only friend. I took Brandy everywhere I went. I kept her in a carrier. I would let her out to eat and use the bathroom but I knew it wasn't fair for her to be stuck in her carrier all the time. So after I dropped her at my cousin's house, I felt relieved knowing she was going to be ok.

I stayed with my aunt for a few days until a guy friend invited me over to his house. He ordered Chinese food & picked it up along the way. I had been to his house once before when we went out on a date. I spent the night there while the next morning he had to go to work. I went with him but I hung out at the stores buying stuff with the money he had given me. After he picked me up, we drove from Lakewood and then to Eatontown, New Jersey. We ate lunch at Popeye's and then he dropped me off at the motel, and purchased the room for me. At the time I had no money. I was penniless and now and trying to figure out what to do.

For the next few days, I started staying at hotels but then had no more money to pay for another room. I thought back to how my cousin, who now had my cat Brandy, said

I could stay with her. I was feeling so fucked up to have to tell her I relapsed earlier and lost my apartment. We talked and she said that I could come back and stay with her. I felt so ashamed and lost but also relieved hearing that I could stay with her. I really didn't want to, but I felt like I had nowhere else to go and no one to turn to. While at my cousin's, I was feeling so depressed. I wondered how things went so wrong. My cousin's house was clean but had lots and lots of roaches and mice. Brandy was catching mice, which made me scared since mice carried rabies. Brandy was a Persian cat. I guess Brandy was also depressed as she stopped using her litter box. It must have been more of a strain, because it was unlike her to do that. I sank deeper and deeper in depression. I would just lay in bed and cry, thinking, "like this shit is rock bottom for me." I couldn't even get my cousin to take me to the store or use her van. I was feeling so fucked right now. It really bothered me because I would never say no to anything she asked of me. I recalled how I would let her borrow my car, anytime she asked. But now, she did not offer anything. My cousin no longer lived in the apartment since she lived with her boyfriend. I was there with her kids and grandkids and did my part when I was there. I cooked and cleaned but nothing was appreciated. One day, she told me that her son was coming home soon so I had to get out of the room I was staying in and sleep on the couch in the living room.

This was tough on me. I had ordered the cable in my name to pay the bill, which would be the way I could pay my way. But she just kept complaining about shit. I ended up missing my appointment with the SA worker so called to make another appointment.

The next morning, I woke up and checked my card and saw I still had food stamps on it. I quickly cleaned up but accidently left some trash. She got so mad and told me that I had to go. I thought to myself, she had 3 grown ass kids in the apartment and no one else could pick up the trash? I recall the phone call I got for her after I had left to go food shopping. She told me not to come back because I didn't pick up the trash. My heart dropped and tears filled my eyes. I thought, "boy when shit hits the fan, it hits hard." I left Brandy there at my cousins while trying to figure out a plan. I went to Long Branch. I thought I would stay the night at my uncle's house. His wife once told me that she would never put me out because she had been homeless before and knew what it felt like. However, my uncle didn't see it that way. He told me I couldn't stay. He made remarks like, "This is no hotel." I couldn't believe how people were acting but I was so fucking angry with myself. I caused this to happen to me, but when people needed me for anything, I never said no. I always helped people when I could. I cried to myself, "why God… why is this happening?" God was showing me the true faces of people. No matter what I ever did for them…I now started to see the different faces of people. Now I was in need of their help and no one was there for me.

I was falling again and it didn't help when my husband called me from a bar and told me to meet him there along with his sister Rose and another friend who I referred to as "Lil Sis." And In my heart, I didn't want to go but went anyway. "Lil Sis" used to be my bestie. They seemed happy to see me but I really wasn't happy to see them at this low point. I thought my husband would have money for me to get high even though I knew they were like everyone else who would talk about me. It would be the same old thing… "Pick on Marlene…" People talk and news travel fast. After a few drinks, they invited me to go to Red Bank to an Elks club bar with them. While we were there, they bought me some more drinks, when tears started falling from my eyes. I was so used to having my own money. It didn't feel right having them buying my drinks. The disease of addiction really changed my thinking. I was very confused.

After leaving the bar, they took me to go get my clothes and my cat from my cousin's house but when we got there, Brandy was nowhere to be found. My heart dropped. Brandy was gone. She was a house cat and couldn't survive outside on her own. How could my cousin do this? I was screaming outside, calling for her but Brandy did not come back. I got some of my clothes and left in tears. The next day, I texted my cousin and asked, "where's my cat?" She claimed she didn't know. We started arguing. I told her I was going to take her to court...she could've called me to tell me to come get my cat... she called me to tell me I couldn't stay there house but never said she would let my cat go if I didn't come get her. At the time, I felt I could never forgive her. It was very mean what she did. I wouldn't ever do that to anyone. I swore that I would never speak to her again.

I ended up going to my husband's sister's house but when she came home from work, she asked me why I was there. I was so upset, quickly left and walked for blocks and blocks. I felt like my legs were going to collapse. My heart felt so heavy and tears were falling uncontrollably. I sat on a bench, crying my eyes out. My husband called me. He came with my friend lil sis and his sister Rose, I'm sitting on a bench crying they came and said don't don't do this!They put me in the car. I was with them for the rest of the day. We went to the store and picked up some food. They then took me back to Lil Sis's house. I got some energy so I cooked, got dressed, went back out to the bar and had a few drinks. I stayed that night at Lil Sis's house, although she really didn't want me to stay there. She seemed mad at me. There wasn't anything I wouldn't have done for her but my addiction had me isolated, to the point where I stopped calling people and stopped answering my phone. At this point I could somewhat understand why she would be upset with me but if you love some like a sister or a friend you would be there for that person. I never harmed or stole from no one. I always had my own shit. I was only able to give her $50.00 in food stamps. I gave it to her to pay my way. I asked her for advice about what to do regarding my charges. I asked her if I should run. Her response was, "no, do not run but handle your problems." But she would not let me stay with her any longer. Boy that was a slap in the face after she just said I could stay with her the night before but I guess that was the alcohol talking. I went back to the welfare worker who asked if I wanted to speak with an SAI worker. I made an appointment and when I went to it, I sat down and told her how I was feeling. From there I thought things were going to move quickly for me to get into a rehab but it was told it would take about 2 weeks after I had to do an intake over the phone. So I went back to lil sister's house and told her I was going to rehab but it was going to take longer than I thought. The night I went back to her house I knocked and rang the doorbell over and over but she did not answer. I saw her bedroom light on and her car was in the driveway, which really upset me. I then went to my husband's sister's house, where my husband now resided. As I approached the door, I called and asked her to open the door. I had to swallow my pride and ask her, she said I could stay. I felt some relief when she said I could but not for long. I knew she didn't like me or at least I felt that way because she was mad at me from when my husband was in the hospital and I barely came to see him and also because I slept with his friend James, never knowing at the time they were friends and my husband and I had been apart during that time. Haven't been together quit for some time but we always looked out for each other, so my aunt comes over my husband sister donna house and say to me, you can't be over this lady house eating and sitting and not speak to her so after that I started speaking to her and every night I asked can I stay the night she said yeah, but I found out that my aunt was paying her for me to stay there when I found out life looked so different I knew my aunt Phyllis had a heart of gold, she would come get me buy me clothes, take me out to eat, that aunt she raise a lot of hell but she'll give you the shirt off her back.

I called bail reform cause I was suppose to report to take a urine every other week I never went not once, I told them I couldn't make it they going to have to lock me back up, cause I had no money to get there and I have a bad back, they said no we don't want to lock you up they gave me their fax number and asked me to fax over a Dr. note so I did I never been nor went to freehold NJ didn't have to give no urine I knew if I went and my urine was dirty it was a done deal for me!

A little voice entered my mind saying why? What is here!? What is left here? You have to go! You have to leave this place! The day was set for me to go, I was supposed to have went to my daughter Tiarrah house the night before I didn't go I want to get high before I left, so I asked donna can she take me to train station on her was to work she said ok, I made up reason not to get on the train the night before to go to Newark my daughter was suppose to transport me to the rehab

Now I have no money, nowhere or nobody to turn to so I go the person I left & neglected for help my husband has always been my savior, not even then I saw he didn't want to help me and I felt he avoid me, hell he didn't give me money for the marijuana then he shut the door in my face. Everyone turned on me the same people I let use my car when they didn't have one, the same people I helped along my life, and I left no one out. The only two people who really helped me at the time were my Aunt fe-fe and Aunt Tam. My husband's sister didn't like me but she still allowed me to stay at her house, so I go to welfare seeking help cause I'm penniless and homeless. They really didn't want to help me because I lost everything.

I was at my breaking point and suicide started entering my mind. I really don't think it would've matter to anyone anyhow, I was thinking of every way to kill myself...life was so unfair. Once I got the call, I changed my mind about going into rehab. Now this is the work of God. This is how I know he never left me. This was when I made the decision to let Tiarrah take me to rehab....

ROLLER COASTER STOPPED...

BACK IN THE REHAB –SUMMER 2018

One morning in rehab, I woke up in severe pain as usual, especially with the rain and thunderstorms. I asked one of the girls that I shared a room with to go get the nurse. I was not able to get out of bed. The nurse came running in my room with the CA. Everyone was looking at me. The nurse asked me what was wrong and I explained my situation about my back. I told her I couldn't get out of bed. She looked at me and said, "We don't help with this and if you can't get out of bed then this isn't the place for you." I told her that my SAI worker told me that I would get help here. She replied, "Well we don't have stuff like this... you have to be self-suffering here." She walked out and I slowly climbed out the bed. I didn't have the strength to take a shower. I figured I would wait until later, so brushed my teeth, getting ready for breakfast. They offered eggs and bagels. I gave my bagel away, tired of eating all this bread. I really didn't want to eat the eggs either. I didn't know what they were putting in the food but it became hard to use the bathroom.

I wanted to finish talking to Jesus. I was feeling so alone. I got on my knees and began crying, telling God how alone I felt. Again, tears were pouring down my face as I thought back on how I got here. The people who were supposed to love me unconditionally, like my mom, who had been living with me, never called to say, "Are you ok?" She didn't even call me to wish me happy birthday. Nothing hurt me more. I starting reflected again on my past. Despite everything that I did for my mom after she broke her leg and got evicted because of my twin brothers. I would help her get in the shower, cook for her, while my brothers were in jail facing more time for attacking my mom's next door neighbor. My mom was in denial and felt they did no wrong in her eyes. I asked my mom to help me to pay the rent because I couldn't get enough money at the time to pay it. Her words were, "It's not that I don't want to…" so I never asked again. As long as I had money, a car, drugs and alcohol and friends, I believed I was in control. At this time I felt as though my family, including my own daughter turned on me, even after I helped her and her boyfriend and my grandkids. As I continued to reflect on all of this, I became deeply depressed. I just wanted to sleep and sleep and never get up. How could everyone turn their backs on me like I was nothing?

I really missed Brandy, so deeply.

GROUP THERAPY WITH MICHAEL…

Michael, one of my counselors asked me about "social psychophysical metamorphosis." I replied, "physical metamorphosis means leave me the hell alone." I also wanted to say, "kiss my ass… now there's my philosophy about metamorphosis and the psychophysical part of this shit!" but I refrained. Nevertheless, as the group went on I started really contributing and exploring my feelings, coming to the realization of why I got high. I realized that one of the reasons stemmed back to the mental and physical pain of when my daughter's boyfriend hit me on my head with a chair.

By the next day, when it was time for the group, I felt really drained from all of the sharing I did the day before. I decided on this day that I would not share this time, not at all. I shut down completely. Apparently, it looked to my counselor that I was sleeping through the session. As I went up to the desk to ask for sugar, Michael walked up to me and asked, "What is your hypothesis on being clean?" I replied, "recovery." Michael seemed surprised. He must have thought I wasn't asleep after all. i just wasn't interested in his group anymore

At about lunchtime, I received a phone call from Mr. D the counselor Mrs. Mayline was a CA at the rehab and she was really nice. She loved when I would do my "lil hookup" - soup and apple pie i would take cut apples sugar and werther's original caramel candy sautee them in the microwave, put bread in the little cups and put it back in the microwave that I would make in the microwave. There was my apple pie"Gggish," I thought I was in trouble for sleeping during the group. Mrs. Mayline asked me to come to the front desk. I became more worried that I was now really in trouble. All types of thoughts were going through my head for a few seconds. It's crazy how many things your mind can do in a few seconds. I slowly got on the phone and waited a minute. I asked Mrs. Mayline, "The phone for you-Marlene?" (in the rehab you don't get any personal phone calls.) She replied, "Yeah!" She said pick up the phone, so i did it was Mr. D telling me that he was going to help me get in a halfway house, my 28 day came and left, At first no one would listen to me,

Two weeks prior, I had created a debate about planning a special activity for us clients. One of the clients thought of doing a talent show but I came up with the idea of doing a fashion show. To think, I won the debate! I won! I just couldn't believe it because I NEVER won anything, except for a scratch-off once! I never had a chance. I never had the chance to play sports. I never really had a chance to be a kid. When the day came for the fashion show, things got even better. We went outside during our cigarette breaks and played all these childhood games like "Red Light, Green Light," "Simon Says," "Duck, Duck, Goose." Having everyone participate in the fashion show and spending the whole day getting it together was a gift. Emotion erupted because I had a moment of being a child. It was amazing to see how we all participated in the fun, from the models to the make-up artists, hairdressers, judges and the audience. I gave special thanks to the CAS for allowing us to come together like this and the greatest thing it wasn't no one arguing, we actually all came together.

REALITY OF REHAB

Sometimes the reality of being in rehab really set in. It became even worse one day after breakfast when one of the ladies got caught with a broken bracelet. Someone reported her, saying she had a weapon. She was getting kicked out of the rehab. I was so upset because it was clear to me that she really wanted to change her life around and now she was being kicked out onto the streets. She and I would always talk and share a lot. I went to the CA and asked if there was anything we could do for her. The CA told me, "no." Prior to this day, we ate at the same table and I couldn't help but get close to some people like her, who shared the same challenges as I did. Seeing her leaving made me speechless and very sad. All I wanted to do was cry. I couldn't believe I was seeing this. I worried for her and wondered what would happen to her. She could die and no one would care. It made me wonder and I was angry about what type of a place would let this happen... Before she left, I hugged her and gave her a pamphlet pleading with her to go to meetings. I told her not to let this disease win...and to get help... go to N.A or A.A meetings. At this point, hearing that when girls leave, overdosing became really serious, more serious than I imagined.

Mrs. Mayline was the one of the CA'S on duty. She walked up to me and said if it was up to me I'd give her another chance and she complimented me on trying to help her and stand up for her. After she left, other girls came to me and accused her of stealing. I thought to myself, maybe they suspected this, but to just kick her out was something I couldn't understand. This is the reason people come to rehab: to get help. It was still nice that Mrs. Mayline acknowledged me trying to help this lady and said it was heartfelt. I didn't know what to say but thank you. It still didn't solve the problem. She was still gone, out to be on the streets.

Being at rehab made me realize that I myself had been a mess for quite some time and that I really didn't know how to ask for help. All my life, everything was always shoved under the rug. For as long as I could remember, I was always depressed thinking of suicide and all types of ways to kill myself. I always felt I was a failure always and would ask God, "why am I here." I guess I never sat still enough to hear him. The rage, the anger and anxiety...all came to light at rehab. While at rehab, I was diagnosed with depression and bipolar disorder. Before I went, I would always find myself crying for no reason, which made me get even more. I just didn't want to feel any pain. I just didn't care what was going on around me. I had times of my life when men would hit on me, trying to sleep with me. I would say, "Stay in lane and wait until it's your turn." This just wasn't normal, but I loved it. I felt that I had some type of control. The control made me feel important... even women would try to sleep with me. I didn't mind that either. I would always think they trying to give me something, something I can't get rid of like AIDS or SYPHILIS but in my head, I didn't want that...

I didn't understand some of the lessons presented to me... "Admit it - that we are unmanageable and powerless." I thought, "Fuck yea... trying to manage an unmanageable life and admitting we are powerless." How do you do that when the drug takes over? These thoughts made me angry.

I also was angry because I felt like my counselor wasn't helping me. I didn't understand what was happening to me. This anger turned to rage and I became scared for myself. At one time in my life I was a harmless, fun, party girl. I went to the Dr. and told him how I was having these crazy thoughts, and feeling more depressed. I recognized I needed help.

In time I learned that when we become part of N.A. We join society of addicts like ourselves, a group of people who know that we help one another as recovering addicts.

These thoughts made me start thinking. I'm here for some reason. There was a lesson that I had to learn. I have always been thinking and feeling like I was a failure and could never hold down a job. I've always had great ideas but it had been hard to accomplish the. I had started to find myself and realized that I had some bad ways. It was then that I realized I had to learn how to turn them to be right with truth and honesty. I asked myself, how could I be honest and truthful to others if I haven't been truthful and honest to myself? God is really starting to show me the steps. I know it was him that led me to this safe place. I now started to understand that I couldn't do anything without God. He became the first man I would say good morning to (LOL)! I started asking him to be with me at all times. After doing this, I began finding myself happy & joyful. People started coming up to me just for a positive conversation.

Even when I had some off days and was down, like for not having any more cigarettes or when my daughter had to cancel her visit with me, I thought to myself, I still got God. I'm going to be OK…

I did really want to see my daughter Tiarrah since the last visit was nice. The waiting to see her was hard for me.

On another day at rehab, one of the girls left and I prayed, God please watch over her.…step with her as she continues to walk the right path…hoping that the next step she would take was to NA or A.A. Thank you Jesus.

Then I thought about another one of the other girls, Karen. She had cried to me the day before and she was still on my mind. I felt so bad for her and just prayed for her.

MS. STEWART'S GROUP…

On one day, we played music in Ms. Stewart's group. Ms. Stewart was a counselor who stuttered and she had this problem since she was a young child. She even stopped talking during her childhood because she was so embarrassed and other kids used to tease her. She decided to go to speech therapy and not let it get the best of her. She decided to claim her life. As an adult, Ms. Stewart still stuttered but not that bad. I loved her group. Unfortunately there were times when the group didn't go as smoothly when one of the girls was bullying some of the others. She would laugh and talk while others were trying to share and it got to the point where some of them stopped sharing because of her. I ended up getting in a heated argument with her for this. I got into her face and wanted to know how on earth could she come to rehab and act in this clique-like way, her and other woman would make funny jokes about my soup saying my soup looked like throw up. On other days, in group, I said to her, "Yeah that's why y'all keep coming back. Y'all go back out to use because you are missing something that you didn't hear nothing the last time you was here cause this a joke to you, there could be a message that someone needs to hear to save their lives and it funny to you.." I said, "You need to thank god you can walk back in these doors, some people can't.. because they're dead." I've been bullied as a kid and i be damned if ima be bullied in a rehab everyone was on my side she got up and left out of the group.we continued with group and it was fun when we listened to music and she would dim the lights. The music she played was inspirational. Ms. Stewart's group taught me a great lesson, "to let go and let God." This resonated with me. It taught me that I couldn't keep dwelling on the same situation. I learned if I keep allowing the devil in and take over my spirit with negativity, I would always be stuck and lost. I also learned I would feel free if I let go of the anger. I began feeling like never before. I felt as if Jesus was working behind the scenes for me. I learned how to separate myself from negative people.

I also began wanting to give back and help. When one of the women in our group got sick, I made soup for her. I could tell this made her happier.

When one of the other girls in our group got discharged I felt really bad for her, especially when she was crying. She got discharged from an offense and had nowhere to go. She got caught saving medication, which she gave to another girl. She called her mother & sister and they wouldn't take her. My heart went out for her, despite her mistake. I often wondered what she was doing now hoped she was hanging on, and didn't end up dead.

PEACE OF MIND & ENERGY

A NEW DAY BEGINS ...WHILE IN REHAB

This one morning, I woke up with my mouth so dry from the medication I had been taking. I ran to the bathroom to throw water in my mouth and then brushed my teeth. I never felt like I got enough sleep while in rehab. It was hard getting used to having to keep up with the demands of adhering to various schedules while in rehab.

Later that day, while in group, we talked about asking for forgiveness, whether we actually robbed or stole from others, even if it was stealing people of time, energy or peace of mind. We prayed for our families and prayed for loved ones that were on the street. We feared that many of them might be getting high and even overdosing/dying.

LEARNING EMPATHY...

There was one counselor that really annoyed me. Something about her disposition and attitude got under my skin. However, I decided to have the mindset that I brought myself to this rehab. I was just passing through to get the tools to stay sober. I decided not to focus on the negative. I was kind of glad that each day I was learning a new little lesson of humility. Each day, I began to plan ways to get help with my medical issues and how I would seek out a better way to get help.

One of the ladies, Mrs. Rhonda was a sweet woman, who cared so little about herself. She would always put herself down and I would tell her beauty comes from within. People may judge others from the outside but it's the inside that is the most important. As I was giving Mrs. Rhonda this advice, I began thinking to myself, "how can I tell someone else this when I care so little about myself and had been destroying my body with drugs and alcohol." This self-realization was an important turning point for me.

During the next morning reflection, we continued a discussion about stealing. It became clearer that a lesson to be learned was that there was a different kind of stealing. I came to realize that when people isolate themselves as I did, from family and friends by not answering the phone or door, I was stealing. My abandonment of family & friends was in a way an act of stealing. This really hit home for me. When I was getting high, I ignored calls from my bank, timeshare, landlord but even worse, from family and friends. I never called back and didn't care.

My eyes kept opening wider after attending more groups. In one group in particular, I learned about the challenges of relationship with friends & and men. In the past, I had a lot of trouble establishing positive relationships. Through the group, I learned that I had to build a relationship with my higher power first. This concept became a big part of my recovery. Just as important, I learned that I needed to wait on God to put the right people in my life.

It came to surface that I wasn't sure how to love. One minute I was in love and then, the next, I wanted to be separated. I learned I didn't really even know who I was. Growing up, I wasn't really loved so it was very hard to know what love really is. I learned that I might have a clearer vision of love if I could stay clean and sober.

I learned that we could ask our higher power (in my case, Jesus) to guide us and rebuke whatever negativity comes our way. I also learned to use the Bible as my guide. I learned that whatever our higher power maybe, we may have a long road ahead, so it is important to keep asking our higher power to guide us and give us strength. I learned that whatever I can't handle, to ask my higher power to take it away from me, so I can move forward and be free minded. I learned that my higher power-Jesus would not give me anything I can't bear. I learned to trust that he knows what I can and cannot do. I learned that faith is as small as a mustard seed. I learned to be so grateful and joyful that I'm finding myself. I became so hopeful for the first time in my life.

Although I began gaining hope, I still had to live day by day in the rehab until I would be recommended and ready to leave. One particular day, I spoke with one of the CA's about how we did not have enough food. I then put a slip tine the suggestion box that we call the food bank and ask them to donate some snacks for us. It worked! Snacks were donated and they were real snacks, not just saltine crackers! We had pretzels and blue chips and yogurt. This was a little life victory.

While in rehab, I finally realized what some of my triggers were including family issues and the car accident I was in. I also learned my relapses included weight gain. I loved to cook and eat food, especially when I was bored. Food, snacks, chips, ice cream, and fast food became my best friend for a while. I began desiring to learn how to maintain more healthy eating habits. I also came to realize my struggles with exercise. When it came to exercising, I used to get discouraged because I didn't see results right away. Coming to these realizations made me more determined to stay away from cocaine and also to make healthier life choices relating to food and exercise. I was finally able to say, forget the drugs. I won't let you get the best of me. This is when I began using the Serenity Prayer to guide me and give me strength…I began saying this prayer over and over again…. "God grant me the Serenity to accept the things I cannot change, the Courage to change the things I can and the Wisdom to know the difference."

I knew now that if I used drugs or alcohol, nothing good would come out of it for me. I had recognized that I was a work in progress! I learned to wait patiently and that program really works for me. I learned I could get beside myself. I heard people say, "Don't leave until the miracles happen." I was going to find out what the miracle was!

ANOTHER STEP LEARNED IN PROGRAM….

In step 5, I learned we have to admit our wrongs to God and others we hurt. While using, I totally could not admit the wrong I did for my husband. I lied, cheated, not with another man, but for not being there when he needed me most. However, I also realized that although he tried to be there for me when I needed him as a friend, I could no longer endure his mental and physical abuse. I should've divorced him first. Despite it all, I still cared about him but now understood that I can't be with someone who was an abuser. I realized I had been talking to other guys because I was lonely and looking for friendship. I realized how sorry I was for not being there for my kids like a mother should've been. Being in rehab helped me to see how my disease of addiction had me bound. While in rehab, I saw girls leaving and then learned how some of them went back out there and died. Even some of the CA's were recovering addicts. I recalled crying after hearing one of the CA's stories of how after doing 8 years in prison; she got her life together but while doing her son died in her arms. She talked about the challenges of building up relationships with her kids because of the damage she had done. This was what I needed to hear. This allowed me to think that this could or could've been me... no one is invincible to this disease called addiction.

ANOTHER SPARK OF HOPE
THROUGH PRAYER....

Another day went by. That morning when I woke up, I did a little meditation and said a prayer to Jesus. While meditating, I began to cry thinking about so many things. I thought about my lost cat Brandy and asked God to please help me find her. I pleaded for my kids and me to have success in all areas in our lives. I then pleaded for God to never leave me. I knew I couldn't do anything without him. It felt so great to pray to him and praise his name. I guessed my faith was not strong enough when I first started praying... I hadn't been able to find the words to ask for his help. But now, once again I was asking him why he keeps saving me? Only he knows.

LINDSAY LEAVES REHAB...

PLAN TO GET TO HALFWAY HOUSE....

I had to meet with my counselor, who was not someone I related too well with. She wanted to know every detail of what we were doing while in rehab and our plan for after. I was really upset when she said I couldn't go into a halfway house because my back was messed up. It would be hard for them to place me in a halfway house because you had to be self- sufficient. I had to prove them wrong because if I could go to a halfway house, I could start looking for work. Every chance I got, I started working out going in the weight room and often walked the hallways when we were allowed to have free time. I wasn't going to take no for an answer. I was stretching and doing yoga every day. It didn't seem like my counselor was trying to help so I asked to speak with Mr. D, another counselor. When I pulled him aside and explained to him what was going on between me and my counselor, I told him a was going to grievance. Mr. D didn't think I should do that at first. I thought, "ok, PATIENCE!" But nothing happened. I requested to see the director and called my daughter Tiarrah to let her know what was going on. I wasn't aware of my daughter calling as well. I went to the director's office and she got really nasty with me. I wanted to curse her out so bad but I held back. I couldn't believe how she was belittling my daughter and me. However, once they realized that my 28th day had come and gone, I saw Mr. D when he came down to have group after group i said see i'm still here that's when he said i'm listening a week later he took me over to his office and began calling halfway houses and set up some interviews for me. At first, no one contacted me back and another week went by... I heard nothing but he said he was still trying. In the meantime he made me promise that I will complete whichever halfway house I entered because he was putting his neck out for me. I promised! I knew there were so many things that could go wrong in a halfway house and that all types of test would come my way. I had already heard stories about the halfway houses, how girls would bring drugs in. Questions entered my mind... "Am I or will I be strong enough for this?" "Will GOD test my faith?" I had to be ready to put my armor on. I figured I needed the halfway house. I also knew that once at the halfway house, I could start looking for a job and an apartment and wouldn't have to be around anyone using drugs. continuing to live life on life's terms, i really had no clue what life have for me from this day on all i know is that i needed to get into this halfway house, i really don't know all i know is something is leading me there i'm not sure why!i'm actually scared to work or even go up and down stairs taking this leap of faith is like jumping out the window.

AFTER DAYS OF WAITING, GOOD NEWS ARRIVES...

I was now on day 41 and still in rehab. We had a special guest that came in and played his guitar and sung his inspirational music. At the end, he left CDs for everyone. His music really moved me. He was once an addict himself but was now in recovery. When he came he said to me your still here, I replied yes, On that same day, I got a phone call from Mr. D. He didn't disclose everything to me but said my counselor would talk to me but it was good news. Later that day, when my counselor came in, she said, "Marlene, you will be going to the Real House in Bloomfield." I was so happy and even happier when she told me to pack my things since I would be leaving the next morning.

That night, I tossed and turned because I was so excited. Even my CA was excited for me.

I was now ready to go to the next part of my journey from the rehab to the halfway house. I now knew that each day I would have a new chance to experience strength and gain hope. I needed the fellowship of NA.

I had joined the bond of recovery. From the isolation of our addictions, we can find a fellowship of people with a common bond of faith, strength and hope from sharing our experiences. The "admit no weakness," "conceal all shortcomings," "deny every failure," and the "go it alone" approach was the "creed" that I and many other addicts followed. We denied that our lives had become unmanageable, despite all evidence to the contrary. Many of us would not surrender without the assurance there was something worth surrendering to. Many of us took our first step only when we had evidence that addicts could recover in NA. In NA, I was able to find others who've been in the same predicament, with the same needs. These addicts were willing to share with us the tools that worked for them. They were willing to give us the emotional support we needed as we learned to use these tools. From being at rehab and now going to the halfway house, I learned through NA that recovering addicts know how important the help of others can be because they've been given help.

I began to find that in recovery, all doors began to open for me. I would now have many choices and my new life in recovery would be rich and full of promises. While I was taught we couldn't forget the past, we don't have to live in it. We can move on. I would pack my bags and move out of my past into a present filled with hope. Letting go of the past "It is not where we were that counts but where we are going"

I learned that although when we first find recovery, some of us feel shame or despair at calling ourselves "addicts" in the early days, we may be filled with both fear and hope as we struggle to find new meaning in our lives. The past may seem inescapable and overpowering. It might make us think of ourselves in a new way other than the way we always have.

However, I learned that memories of the past could serve as reminders of what's waiting for us if we use again. On the other hand, they can also keep us stuck in a nightmare of shame and fear. Though it may be difficult to let go of those memories, each day in recovery can bring us that much further away from our active addiction.

After losing everything, I knew that not showing up to follow through would've been another disappointment. I already felt such guilt, shame, and stupidity. I had felt like a failure because most of all, I failed myself. In the past, the only things I knew how to do were run, hide and isolate. But no more. I have stayed on the path of recovery. I made the decision to follow through with the plan God made for me.

Hi, my name is Marlene C and I'm An Addict!

I loved getting high on crack cocaine. I loved men and the attention I got. I was a daredevil, living life on the edge and fell but I have been able to get back up with a few minor bumps and bruises. I was able to rise! I have learned to live a new way of life without mind-altering chemicals.

It had to have been God's will to keep me in rehab for those 42 days. He must have had a purpose for me. I did not go to rehab with the intention of making friends but I did. God let me see people for who and what they were. I learned many lessons. Some of the people left rehab and died. I saw different faces of many different people who challenged me on the decisions and choices I had to make. In some ways, this allowed me to become stronger. I learned that all the challenges and dilemmas in life will still be there and no one can say it will be easy. But I also learned ways that I could now begin dealing with the challenges life will keep bringing. Getting along with family, friends, co-workers and keeping jobs and even dealing with death can become reachable goals if I take accountability for my own actions.

As I reflect back to the 28th day I was in rehab, I recall how I was thinking, "Why me?" But now after 42 days, I asked, "Why not me?" I learned to stop going on my own understanding. After fighting really hard to get into a halfway house even when my counselor told me I wouldn't be eligible, I didn't give up. And thankfully, one man, Mr. D, believed in me and somehow made it work. I'll never forget his phone all and his words to me, "Marlene, you are on your way!" After hearing these words, it was then that I realized there has to be something way beyond me! I have always believed in God but didn't think he was with me. But at this time, I knew God has always been with me. This time, I would surrender my own ways and try to let God take over.

In the end we never know what becomes of us. I'm hoping whoever will read this will know there is a message of hope. The time is now to teach your child or children about staying away from drugs and its just as important as teaching them about sex and the dangers of abductors, predators and stranger danger. The number of deaths relating to drugs keeps rising. Do not lose your families to this addiction. There is an epidemic outside your doors and do not hide what is going on in the real world. Kids are dying every day to this addiction. It doesn't hurt to have your child or children hear this message in school but its better when it is coming from home. Sometimes you may wonder if once your child leaves home, will they ever return? Try to reach out to the right people when you feel the need.

I was in rehab for a reason. GOD helped me open my eyes and my heart. I don't ever want to come back or go back to that place called darkness. There were so many trials and tribulations in my life that contributed to my addictions but it doesn't have to be that way anymore. I don't need to use drugs and alcohol in an attempt to escape from life. At times, I still feel depressed and wonder why I didn't die. Why does GOD continue to save me? I am not sure but have a new chance to find out.

Everyone has a story. Mine is different than yours, but one thing we have in common is that we are all addicts in one form or another. The question is, how will we manage our addictions so we can live a happy, productive and peaceful life. I am a work in progress. I've seen and experienced many different faces through this course of my life, now I'm on my new journey of different faces.i'm managing my pain, overcame my past life and still i have a long road ahead of me, This is only the beginning i've been bullied, kicked at, i was told that i was belligerent, girls even made front of my soups and my apple pie, but toward the end they were all saving their desserts from lunch and dinner so i can make desserts out of jello, apple chocolate chip cookie, yup they were freely handing it over, In this rehab i've seen people come and go, i heard of people dying, i've seen people escape, i've seen and witnessed girls getting kicked out and had no place to go or no one to turn too, is this what god wanted me to see that he wanted to get me alone so i can see and witness and to pay attention to what he wanted me to do he wanted me to see that he saved me from self destruction, coming to this rehab wasn't the best as i thought in the beginning it opened my eyes, i didn't, even know that i was safe from the courts well at least for now i'm safe, even the girls that left before me that went to halfway houses some went home, even the girls i had issues and argument. with i hugged them all and wished them farewell along their journeys they looked at me like i was crazy one girl jumped back she was so shocked i hugged her.This let me see that life is too short. God let me see that i'm not in a jail cell and the best of all, i'm writing to maybe save someone to help somebody, i'm writing because i'm not dead..I'M ALIVE..i have a chance to start over! Once you're dead you can't start over, you can't say WAIT! Give me another chance, it's too late! LET HOLD HANDS AND TOGETHER WE STAND from one addict to another it doesn't matter what your drug of choice is or was, remember we're all addicts in one form or another, just because you may never used a drug or even drinked alcohol don't ever think life can't sweep you off your feet cause you are an addict too! we're all addicted to something! We just have to admit that our lives have become powerless and unmanageable. We can all start right there, just take a good look at yourself in the mirror, what does your reflection tell you, sometimes we have to reflect a little deeper and or take a deeper look you can't ever forget where you came from or where we've been in our lives. You can't hide it, you can't run from it face it head on, some people are afraid to face their addictive behaviors.Life has a way of showing up! HOW WILL YOU HANDLE IT>>THIS THING CALLED LIFE! you are in control of your own life, it is your decision where you want to go from here..remember this SKIES THE LIMIT!! What's your journey{SMILE} I think I'm starting to smile more!

That's why I say the serenity prayer, we have no control of what is going to happen, but what we can control is how we endure life situations.

Printed in the United States
By Bookmasters